The Llamas OF ShangriLlama

Written by Sharon "Mama Llama" Brucato • Illustrated by Patrick Williams

First Edition

Happy Trails from Mama Llama!

7 Day Health Publishers, Yorba Linda, California

The Llamas of ShangriLlama
© 2012 by Sharon Brucato
First Edition

Published by:
7 Day Health Publishers
Yorba Linda, CA 92886 U.S.A.
www.7dayhealth.com

Distributed by: www.ShangriLlama.com

Illustrated by: Patrick Williams
www.pwilliamsart.com

All rights reserved. No part of this book may be reproduced or transmitted in any form or by any means, electronic or mechanical, including photocopying, recording or by any information storage and retrieval system, without written permission from the author, except for the inclusion of brief excerpts in a review.
Printed in Mexico.

Library of Congress Control Number: 2012913933

Summary: Tommy has to learn about llamas from head to toe before his mother will buy a pack of llamas for their new farm called ShangriLlama.

Publisher's Cataloging-in-Publication Data
(Prepared by Quality Books Inc.)

Brucato, Sharon.
The Llamas of ShangriLlama / Sharon Brucato; illustrated by Patrick Williams.
P.cm.
ISBN-13: 978-0-9772219-1-2

1. Children's Nonfiction   2. Animals   3. Llamas   4. Rhyming Books

Some kids like dogs and cats; others like less common pets, such as ferrets and giant snakes. My son Tommy likes...llamas! What a journey our family has been on to learn about, select and make a home for a pack of funny, furry llamas. This book is dedicated to you, Llama Boy, for introducing such mesmerizing animals to our family.

Love,
Mama Llama

To his surprise, his mom replied, "First find out where they're from, and also learn about their needs, and then let's purchase some!"

So Tommy used the Internet
to learn what others knew.
He also phoned a llama vet,
a breeder and a zoo.

Tommy did discover next
how very odd, indeed,
that llamas are from head to toe.
His mom begged, "Please, proceed!"

He started with the llama's ears that look just like bananas and turn front and back, out and flat like dancing ballerinas.

The eyes! They're bulging shiny globes,
well shaded from bright light
by a horizontal stripe of black—
and still they have great sight.

Their upper lip is split in two and used like fork and spoon to nimbly pick up bits of hay to eat or spit at you!

They spit because they love to eat
and never want to share.
When other llamas take their food
spit happens, so beware!

Llamas have a tiny tongue,
quite narrow and light pink.
It barely sticks out half an inch!
To see it, you can't blink.

Their wooly, soft and gorgeous coats
are black, white, brown or gray,
or solid, spotted—patchwork, too!
This wool is sheared each May.

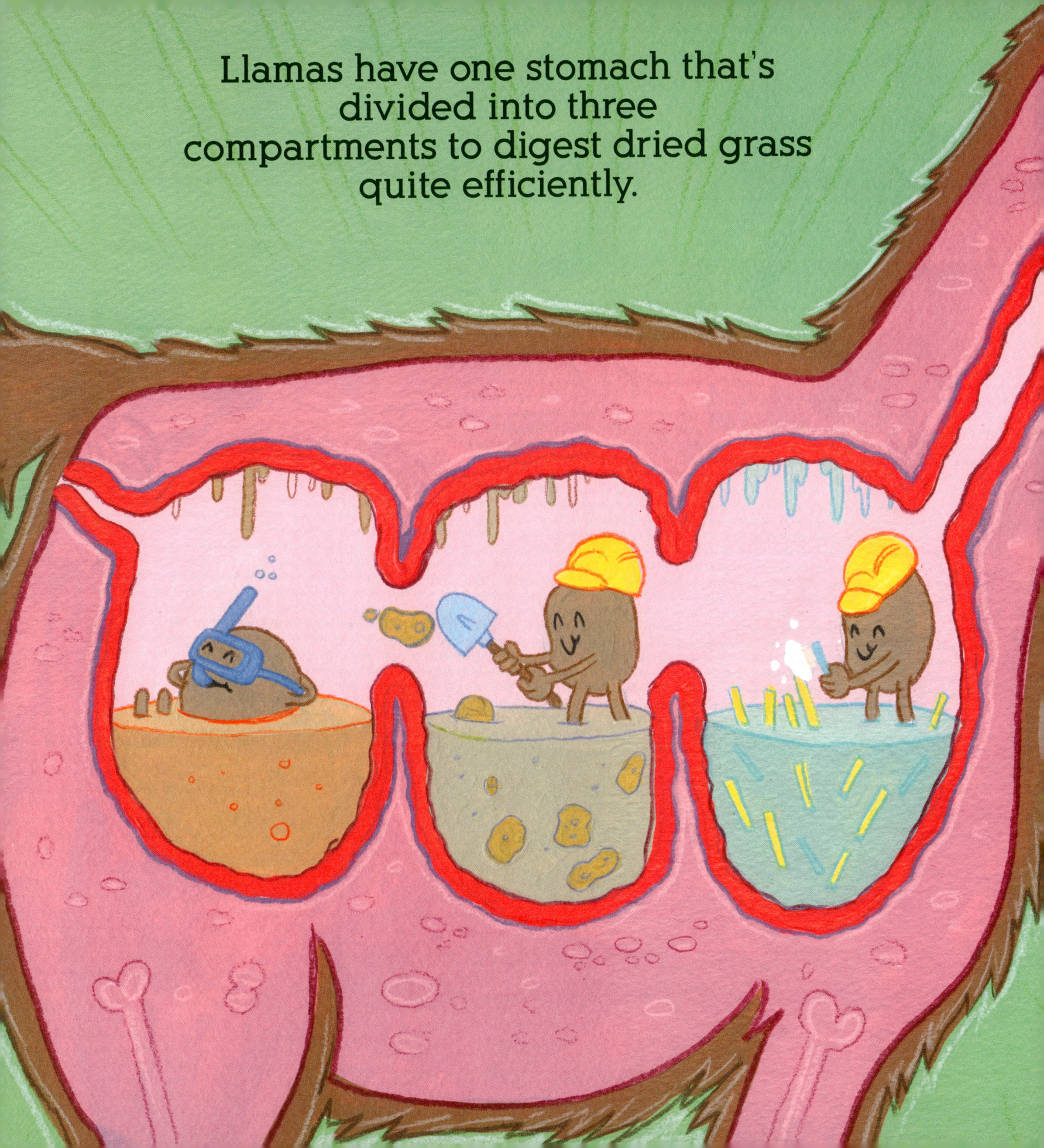

In fact, the grass turns into beans
inside the llama's belly.
The beans are small— like rabbit poo—
and they're not even smelly!

Llama legs are long and thin,
which makes them oh-so-fast.
In a race, they'd tie a deer
but beat the tall giraffe.

With just two toes and padded soles,
the llama's foot is gentle
on trails and hills and grassy fields—
they're so environmental!

Tommy's mommy was impressed
by all those llama facts.
So she and Tommy drove to farms
that raised big llama packs.

They bought five llamas from those farms
and brought them home to graze
in grassy fields with shade and stalls.
The neighbors were amazed!

They asked, "What are the names you chose for your five quirky pets?" Tommy laughed then told them what he calls his odd quintet.

Pajama Llama is the one whose coat is black and white. As leader of the llama pack, he guards them day and night.

Bahama Llama's brown and white,
and he is overweight.
He loves big hugs and kisses, too!
With children he's first rate.

The youngest member of the pack
is named Como T. Llama.
This spunky, spotted yearling
lives for llama melodrama.

Tommy and his mommy then named their new llama home. They called it ShangriLlama Farm where five cute llamas roam.